WHAT ARE YOUR WORDS WEARING?

HOW TO MAKE YOUR SALES COMMUNICATIONS COMPREHENSIVE, SUBSTANTIAL, AND PRECISE

JOHN KURTH

outskirtspress
DENVER, COLORADO

Introduction:
About the Author

John is the President and Founder of **Syntactics Sales Scripting®**: *The Syntax of Success*®, that helps sales managers and individual sales people create winning sales scripts that close sale-after-sale-after-sale!

John Kurth has more than 12 years of combined international sales experience in Hong Kong, Taiwan, and the United States.

He has written winning Sales Scripts in the following industries:

- Insurance
- Financial Services
- Computer/IT
- Health Care
- Security
- Logistics, and
- Network Marketing.

John has a *Master's Degree in Business Administration* (International MBA) and an undergraduate degree in *History*.

John is married to Josephine; they have a beautiful daughter, named Rita. John also enjoys strategy games like playing chess, reading books, and enjoying the great outdoors. John has been an active member of <u>Toastmasters International</u> for more than 10 years.

Table of Contents

Welcome

Dear Sales Executives and Business Owners,

I want to acknowledge you today for taking the time to invest in the success of your sales team and your business!

As a Top Sales Executive or Sales Professional, you're always looking for ways to improve sales productivity, streamline your sales processes, and lead your sales team to new levels of success.

Whether you are a Sales Executive or Sales Professional, by implementing these strategies in this book, you will rapidly transform your career!

Success Exercises

This is both a textbook and a workbook. You will find Success Exercises throughout this book. When you come across an exercise, grab a pen and complete the exercise! People who take action are rewarded! Challenge yourself to complete the exercise before you go onto the next chapter. Invest at least 10 minutes to complete an exercise before going on to the next chapter.

Let's jump right in and get started!

CHAPTER 1

What Is Scripting and How Can It Help Me?

What is Scripting?

What are *Sales Scripts*?

Why should you care?

What *Scripting* is <u>NOT</u>:

First, let's define what *Scripting* is <u>not</u>.

Scripting is not speaking like a robot!

Scripting is not rigid!

Scripting is not manipulative!

What *Scripting* Is:

Scripting is being authentic to who you are. Your real personality shines through. Your unique selling-style is enhanced. You are more confident and can listen better to potential customers, and you can be more successful in winning more customers.

The Definition of a *Script*:

Let me share with you the definition of a *Script*.

The definition of a *Script* is:

"Words in sequence that have meaning."

If you are talking and making sense, you are using a *Script*. If you are talking and not making sense, you are talking in gibberish. *"Mumbo, dogface, banapatch" is* gibberish. It doesn't make any sense! So the question is not whether you are using a *Script* or not, the question is:

"Are my Scripts as powerful and persuasive as possible?"

Let me ask you a question:

"Would you rather be occasionally brilliant or consistently excellent?" An amateur sales person is occasionally brilliant and wonders "What happened? Why did I make the sale?" A successful sale for the amateur sales person is an event, an almost random occurrence because the salesperson is not aware of what he is doing.

Let's contrast the above situation with the "consistently excellent" sales professional. A consistently excellent sales professional embraces *Scripts*, uses *Scripts*, and has

become the *Scripts*. The scripting is at such a high level that the *Scripts* are virtually invisible to the prospect. That is why sales professionals consistently win customers and close sale-after-sale-after-sale.

Sales professionals focus on their *Scripts* as part of the *Sales Process*. You improve the inputs in the *Sales Process* and make more sales or better *Outputs*. A sales professional knows he has the most influence on the *Sales Process*, which leads to the outcome he desires, namely, making a sale.

That is why sales people, who are new to their profession and struggling, marvel at the top producers. They think that the top-producers are "just born that way." This is a **MYTH**! Selling is a learned skill, and top-producing sales people became that way because they continually work on their sales skills, and one of the most important sales skills that a sales person needs to master is *Sales Scripting*. You can model top-producing sales people and become even more successful. One of the key processes that top-producing sales people work on is the *Scripts* they use. In the visual age of TV and the Internet, many people have forgotten the power of the spoken word.

The words you use and the scripting techniques make all the difference between a missed opportunity and a sale.

World-class *Scripts* are:

- Comprehensive

- Substantial, and
- Precise.

Comprehensive

Your *Scripts* must reflect your industry-knowledge AND your unique selling style. No two sales people sell in the same way. That's why there is no "one way" to sell because if the *Script* does not reflect your unique selling style, it will feel "inauthentic", and the *Script* will not be used. Once you stop following the *Script*, you are *winging-it* and getting *wing-it* results.

Substantial

Your *Scripts* must be substantial. There must be plenty of "meat" in your *Scripts*. Not just "fluff." The substance or the "meat" involves benefit-driven language and compels the person to take action and buy; furthermore, there are more than 100 different *Scripting* techniques that can be embedded to make your sales presentations more powerful and persuasive.

Precise

Your *Scripts* must be delivered with precision. Precision involves **focus**, **timeliness**, and ***repeatability***.

Focus

Every word and every phrase in your *Script* must be evaluated. Does the word or phrase need to be included in the *Script*? If not, delete it, or do you need to add some more material?

Timeliness

This leads to *Timeliness*. Your delivery must be timely. Just enough time to make the sale and not a moment longer! This is respectful of your prospect's time and your time as well. If a sales person's current presentation is 60 minutes long, he can only deliver a maximum of 8 sales presentations per day: however, if he can condense his presentation to 30 minutes, he can now deliver twice as many presentations — 16 per day! Even if his *close-ratio* stays the same, he will still make more money because he is selling to more people. I have worked with clients who have tightened their sales presentations from 60 minutes to 30 minutes, and their close-ratios increase while they are selling to more people.

Repeatability

A key component of precision is *repeatability*. It doesn't matter if the person you are speaking with is your 1st call of the day or your 10th; the potential customer needs you to be as powerful and persuasive as possible because he WANTS a well-delivered sales presentation every time. He wants to make a buying decision, so a well-crafted

Script has the *repeatability* factor. Whether you are tired or not makes no difference! Whether you have had a cup of coffee or not makes no difference! You will be able to deliver your *Scripts* again and again from an authentic place.

You have a choice!

You can resist *Scripts*! You can wing your presentations and get inconsistent results. You can focus on the events. This is a recipe for frustration, low-productivity, and burn-out!

The other option is to embrace *Scripting*. Script every part of your sales process. Make sure your *Scripts* are comprehensive, substantial, and precise.

The Monica Story:

About a year ago, I was referred by a business colleague to an experienced salesperson, named Monica, who had more than five years experience selling insurance for her company. She was doing okay — just making her numbers.

I contacted her, and she said: "*I'm too busy with barely enough time to keep my head above water.*" I politely followed-up with her every couple of months, but she was always too busy to meet. Finally, she agreed to see me.

Near her office, we had coffee outdoors on a sunny afternoon. When I looked at Monica, you could see the tension in her face because she was under a lot of pressure!

She talked about how her boss told her: *"You need to produce more. Just hitting your numbers isn't enough. Being average just doesn't cut it anymore."*

As she told me this, you could see the frustration and worry on her face. We talked a bit more, and then she went back to her office. A few weeks later, I followed up with a phone call to find out how she was doing, but I only got her voicemail. I shared with her an encouraging message. A few hours later I got a call.

It was Monica. I could tell immediately that something was wrong. You could hear the sadness in her voice. She said very slowly: *"I got laid off. If I had only started earlier, things would've been different."*

Don't let this happen to you!

Whether you are brand new salesperson or an experienced one, you must embrace *Sales Scripting* for your long-term success!

CHAPTER 2

Stories

"Baking Bread and Scripting"
5 Secret Ingredients of Winning Sales Scripts

Overview

Have you ever baked bread before? Many of you have. The secret to baking a delicious loaf of bread is to follow a recipe. Many recipes for baking bread include the following ingredients:

- Flour,
- Yeast,
- Water,
- Egg, and
- Salt.

The ingredients for a great *Script* is just like that. If you have a good recipe with the right ingredients and follow the recipe, you'll bake a decent loaf of bread. When you follow the recipe, you'll get *predictable results*.

Today, we are going to start the process of getting the key *Script* ingredients.

Let me share with you the five key ingredients to writing powerful persuasive scripts. This is a process I go through with my clients before I help them with their scripts.

The 5 secret ingredients of winning *Scripts* are:

1. Stories,
2. Benefits,
3. Probing Questions,
4. Objections, and
5. Offer.

Take out a new sheet of paper and at the top write the word "Benefits." There are 5 different types of benefits:

1. Tangible benefits — things you can touch or feel,
2. Intangible benefits (Peace of Mind, Confidence, etc.),
3. Benefits of taking action,
4. Consequences of not taking action, and
5. Benefit of the Benefit.

Take out a new sheet of paper and at the top write the words, "Probing Questions."

Questions help qualify the prospects and help determine their need. No need! No Sale!

Just list the questions you need to ask your clients.

Take out a new sheet of paper and at the top write the word, "Objections."

Every industry has around 7 to 12 common objections. This is good news because you can start developing responses to these common objections. There are 3 ways to handle an objection:

1. Before it comes up,
2. After it comes up, or
3. Ignore it.

Let's talk about the common objections in your industry. Later, write down how you would answer these specific objections. What are other successful sales professionals saying to handle the objection? Write down as many answers as you can to each objection. We'll script your responses to each objection for maximum impact.

Take out a new sheet of paper and at the top write the word, "Offer."

What is your Offer?

How can people do business with you? Is it a 6 month contract? A 12 month contract? Do you accept major credit cards? What are your acceptable forms of payment? Do you have a guarantee or warranty?

Top-Producing Salespeople and Sales Forces have a Success Story LIBRARY.

Top-producers and sales forces have a Success Story Library. Let me explain. Why are stories important in selling? For many reasons. As young children, our parents read to us stories. Stories kept us engaged, and we learned about the world through stories, so we are conditioned to listen to stories. Stories, when told, engage both sides of the brain: the <u>analytical side</u> (left brain) and the _emotional side_ (right brain.) When people hear stories, they tend to lower their resistance. They might think to themselves: "The sales person is just telling me a story." But the story will make selling points.

Types of Stories

There are several types of stories which are a part of every <u>Success Story Library</u>:

- Individual Sales Professional's Story
- Company Story
- Key Product or Service Story
- Success Stories (Testimonials)
- Before and After Stories
- Sales of People Who Did Not Buy Your Product or Service Who Now Regret It.

Sales Professional's Story

Sales professionals need to create their stories that engage listeners. In many industries, like insurance and financial services, sales people are literally the face of the company. Almost all interactions go through the sales person, so the story should build trust, rapport, and confidence.

Company's Story

The company's story is also essential to the sales process and must be included in the Success Story Library. In many instances, there is a compelling story of the founder or the founding of the company. Even if the company is very mature and even global in nature, the company's story is very important.

Mary Kay example

Mary Kay's story is a classic example of the power of the story that is essential to the very identity of the business. When Mary Kay began, it was just her story when she was selling her beauty products, door-to-door. As the company grew, Mary Kay was in a leadership role. The new Mary Kay sales representatives have BOTH their own story about why they got started in the business, and they also tell the story about Mary Kay. A story about the company's founder and the company's vision can be a very powerful asset for your company.

What is your company's story?

Key Product or Service Story

Stories about key products or services are also important — perhaps how the product or service was invented. Think about the story of Velcro. The inventor was walking his dog in the fields one day and had trouble removing the burrs from his clothes. The inventor looked under the microscope at the structure of the burrs and thought he could invent a product that could duplicate the results. He spent years perfecting his idea. The story is still relevant and powerful today, years after the product was released. That is the power of stories because they retain their relevancy and effectiveness for years and even decades.

Success Stories: Testimonials Provide Social Proof

Success Stories are so important because they provide "Social Proof." Social proof is external validation about the quality of the companies' products and services. Social proof lowers resistance which makes the prospects feel that they will not make a bad decision to purchase because people don't want to make a mistake. "Social Proof" reduces the perceived risk of purchasing a product or service. When you're able to reduce the risk, people are more likely to buy.

The Before and After Story

This is a special type of _success story_: "Before and After." "Before and After" stories enable the prospect to imagine what it's like to be a successful user of your service. Think about weight loss ads. Weight loss television

advertisements use the "Before and After" type of story perfectly! The advertisements begin by showing a picture of someone who was very overweight. Then they show a picture of the person after using a weight loss program or product who now looks great! This is a classic example of using a "Before and After" story.

Think about Before and After stories
for YOUR Business!

Success Exercise

This is both a textbook and a workbook. Grab a pen and on the following page list as many stories as you can for your business. People who take action are rewarded! Take your pen and write down at least 10 stories for your business. Challenge yourself to write down 20 stories! Before you go onto the next chapter, invest at least 15 minutes to work on your stories.

Do that now!

Stories

1. _____

2. _____

3. _____

4. _____

5. _____

6. _____

7. _____

8. _____

9. _____

10. _____

11. _____

12. _____

13. _____

14. _____

15. _____

16. _____

17. _____

18. _____

CHAPTER 3

"What Benefits Excite Your Customers?"

Benefits:

What excites your customers? The important word is to *excite*. Your potential customer must feel a connection to the benefit. There must be a thought or a feeling that the benefit will help the prospects solve their problems. *The benefits must be relevant to the prospects needs*. No relevancy, no connection, and, therefore, no sale!

Sales people and sales forces know the five different types of benefits and use them in every single sales presentation.

The 5 different types of benefits are:

- Tangible Benefits,
- Intangible Benefits,
- The Benefits of Taking Action,
- The Consequences of not Taking Action, and

- The Benefit of the Benefit.

Tangible Benefits

Tangible Benefits: things that can be touched, felt, or measured. Make more money or save money. Improvements in performance!

Intangible Benefits

Intangible benefits are things that can't be touched, felt, or measured, but they are very real, for example, peace of mind, confidence, feeling sexy, or having more energy.

Benefits of Taking Action

People will buy today if you give them a reason to buy today. Many sales people lose sales because they don't give the prospect a convincing reason to buy today. The prospect thinks about it and never gets back to making the sale.

Consequences of Not Taking Action

You want to make sure your prospect understands that the cost of doing nothing is also **greater** than the cost of doing something. It's okay to get the prospects connected to the consequences if they do nothing, so you are providing them the solution to their problem.

Benefit of the Benefit

The *Benefit of the Benefit* is one of the most power-ful benefits! Salespeople who can find the *Benefit of the Benefit* and link the product or service to the *Benefit of the Benefit*, then the sales presentation becomes ***very persuasive***. Let me give you an example. There is a financial service professional who is meeting with a young couple with a child who is only three years of age. The Sales Professional demonstrates that he can save the couple $300 a month; that's $3,600 a year. The $300 a month or $3,600 a year is the *Tangible Benefit* of what he is offering. The financial sales professional wants to find the *Benefit of the Benefit*, so he will ask a question in order find out the *Benefit of the Benefit*. *"I can save you $3,600 a year. How would you invest the money?"* The prospect responds: "We could put our child through college without having to take out student loans." This is the *Benefit of the Benefit*.

The Sales Professional will further lock it down by linking the *Benefit of the Benefit* to what he offers. For ex-ample, *"Now imagine you're saving $3,600 a year. You can afford to send your child to the college of his choice without having to take out student loans. What would that feel like?"*

Focus on the Benefits of Most Interest to the Prospect

Focus on benefits of most interest to the prospect, not the benefits of most interest to the sales person. This is a mistake that many salespeople make. Salespeople focus on the benefits of most interest to them, rather than one of most interest to the prospect. Sales people who make that mistake quickly alienate prospects! That is another reason why probing questions are so important! Probing questions often reveal what is of most interest to the prospect, so then the sales professional can tailor the presentation to the prospect.

Benefits are NOT Self-Evident

Most benefits are NOT self-evident! Salespeople must make them explicit or risk losing the prospect. Many salespeople, because they deliver presentations day after day, think the product or service benefits are obvious to the prospect. If they do not make the benefits explicitly clear to the prospect, some prospects will not understand all of the benefits and may choose not to buy. Here's a scripting language to make the benefits very clear: "How *this benefits you is....*"

Use *Benefits* **strategically**. Do you use a shotgun or a rifle? A shotgun sprays shots in a wide angle. A rifle, on the other hand, is precisely targeted. Inexperienced salespeople tend to use *benefits* like a shotgun. They "spray" their prospects with every *benefit* that they can think of and hope a few *benefits* will connect with the prospect. This is inefficient, and you may lose your prospect entirely when using the "spray and pray" method. Rifles on the other hand, are very accurate. You want to use your *benefits* with precision. Choose your *benefits* carefully and weave them into your sales presentation.

Worksheet

This is both a textbook and a workbook. Grab a pen and on the following page list as many benefits as you can for your business. Remember to include all five types of benefits on your list. People who take action are rewarded! Take your pen and write down at least 10 benefits for your business. Challenge yourself!

Benefits

1. _____

2. _____

3. _____

4. _____

5. _____

6. _____

7. _____

8. _____

9. _____

10. _____

11. _____

12. _____

13. _____

14. _____

15. _____

16. _____

17. _____

18. _____

CHAPTER 4

Questions

Question: "Learn How to Control the Conversation"

Powerful Probing Questions

Probing Questions find <u>Needs</u>, <u>Wants</u>, or <u>Desires</u>. Questions help qualify the prospects and help determine their need. No need! No Sale!

What Are Your Seven Key Questions?

Many times, only seven questions are needed in order to help the prospects make a buying decision and discover the needs or wants that they have; you can ask more questions, if necessary. Make sure the salespeople ask enough questions to keep the sales process moving along; however, make sure the sales people are not asking only two or three questions before moving into their sales presentation because they are not spending enough time on this section if they are only asking two or three questions.

Questions Control Focus

It's important to remember that questions steer focus. Sales People lead prospects in a way to help them discover for themselves that they have a need, want, or desire. The questions and the rest of the sales presentation will help prospects determine that the company's solution is the best solution for them.

The following story is about a client of mine, named Carol, who owns and operates a successful art gallery. When prospects would walk through the door, the sales staff did not know how to properly guide them through the process to help them identify what types of art they were interested in. As part of the larger overall sales process, I helped them craft a series of questions to help the prospects narrow down what types of art they would be interested in. Once armed with that knowledge, the sales professional would then guide them through the process of purchasing a fine piece of art.

Picture this in your mind. The prospect walks into the gallery and is greeted by the sales professional. The prospects say they are interested in art, but this is their first time to the gallery, and they are not quite sure where to begin.

Sales professional: *"Are you interested in Sculptures or Paintings?"*

Prospect: *"Paintings."*

Sales Professional: *"Would you be interested in a more*

traditional landscape type of painting or something more abstract?"

Prospect: *"Something more abstract."*

Sales Professional: *"Would you prefer brighter colors or more earthen-tones?"*

Prospect: *"Brighter colors."*

Notice, in three powerful probing questions, the sales person has identified what types of art the prospect is really interested in. Armed with this knowledge, the sales professional will be more powerful and persuasive.

The Right Order and Sequence

Prioritize questions in the right order and sequence. Not only must salespeople ask the right questions, but they must put them into the right order and sequence; for example, in financial services, it is important to know how much money the prospect has to invest; however, if that is the first or second question, *"How much money do you have to invest?"* many prospects would be afraid, and a sale would end right there! Later in the sales process and questioning process, salespeople can ask prospects how much they have to invest. *Questions have timing to them.*

"Easier" questions first. Then "harder" questions.

So, after you have determined what questions you want your salespeople to ask, are going to ask, and when you're going to ask them, the next step is **how** are the sales people going to ask them? Your questions need to be asked as powerfully and persuasively as possible; therefore, you must script your questions.

Probing Questions and Probing Statements

Many salespeople agree that asking questions is a key component in discovering the prospect's needs, wants, and desires that are essential to making the sale. It is the level of detail of the types of questions and asking the questions with precision that separates the average salesperson from a *Top-Producing Salesperson.*

Top-Producing Salespeople write out all the possible questions they would want to ask a potential customer and then objectively choose the most effective probing questions and probing statements to use in their sales presentation. The probing questions and probing statements are then scripted for maximum selling effectiveness. A Top-Producing Salesperson decides, in advance, what is the best order and sequence to ask those probing questions.

Probing questions are pretty self-explanatory, and Probing Statements encourage a prospect to reveal other important information that will help the Top-Producing Salesperson to close the sale.

Here are two examples of probing statements:

1. *"Tell me more about that,"* or
2. *"Describe to me your investment style."*

Qualifying and Disqualifying Questions

As sales professionals, we want to spend as much time as possible with qualified prospects; otherwise, we're wasting our time. It is important to use both qualifying and disqualifying questions to make sure you're wisely spending your time with the qualified prospects. You'll need to create the qualifying and disqualifying questions and customize them for your particular industry.

Example: The 1-10 Scale

How to use the 1-10 point scale:

A colleague runs a <u>Stop Smoking Clinic</u>. Through advanced hypnosis, after one session, people will quit smoking. Forever!

He charges $1,800 for his treatment which is what a smoker would spend each year if he smokes one pack of cigarettes a day. Working with people who want to quit smoking isn't enough! He wants to work with people who are really motivated to quit, so he uses a questioning technique to disqualify the people who say they want to quit smoking but who are not really serious.

This is a very important distinction in selling. *You want to disqualify people who would not be a good fit for your product or service.* When you disqualify the people who are not a good fit, the people you do work with will get better results, be happier, and stay with you longer and when they get great results, you often get referrals and testimonials!

My colleague uses an advanced scripting technique called *__Leading Language__*.

Using *__Leading Language__*, People *__Believe What They Say__*, not What *__You Say__*.

Leading Language is a powerful technique in your scripting toolkit. Why is it so important? **Because people believe what they say**, not what you say. People are inherently skeptical of what other people say, which includes salespeople. People don't deliberately lie to themselves, so if you get prospects to say what you want them to say, it has a deeper level of impact! Here's a quick example: "*If you want to get better at playing the piano, how do you get better at playing the piano?*" The prospect will respond with "You practice." This is the power of *Leading Language*.

Here's how to use the *__Leading Language__* technique with a 1-10 point scale:

"On a scale of 1-10, with 1 being slightly motivated to quit smoking and 10 being you'll do whatever it takes to quit smoking, how motivated are you to quit smoking?"

You only work with people who are 7 or higher on the scale. He disqualifies people who are 1-6 and only works with people who are a 7 or higher. This is a powerful technique that you can use to disqualify people who are not a good fit and only work with people who are most likely to buy your product or services.

Worksheet

This is both a textbook and a workbook. Grab a pen on the following page and list as many benefits as you can for your business. Remember to include *all five types of benefits* on your list. People who take action are rewarded!

Take your pen and write down at least **10 Questions** for your business.

Challenge yourself!

Questions

1. _____

2. _____

3. _____

4. _____

5. _____

6. _____

7. _____

8. _____

9. _____

10. _____

11. _____

12. _____

13. _____

14. _____

15. _____

16. _____

17. _____

18. _____

CHAPTER 5

The Offer

"What Exactly Are You Selling?"

The next secret is to make sure your <u>Offer</u> is written out **word-for-word.** Prospects want to do business with you. If you have done your job properly, the prospect will definitely want to work with you, so don't make it complicated!

The <u>Offer</u> is just explaining the ways you can work together. The information included in this section is price, any guarantees or warranties, any incentives for buying today, or other relevant benefits that can help the buyer make the buying decision. Many salespeople, because they forgot to cover some of the most relevant benefits in the presentation, were not effectively using a script. At this point, introduce new information during the close.

<u>*Do not introduce new information here!*</u>

The Offer is delivered naturally.

The Offer needs to be delivered naturally. Not in a monotone! Salespeople, who have written their Offer word- for-word and have become the script, will avoid the Dr. Jekyll and Mr. Hyde selling syndrome.

The Dr. Jekyll and Mr. Hyde Selling Syndrome:

Let me explain. The Dr. Jekyll and Mr. Hyde selling syndrome happens when the sales person is not properly prepared for the *Offer and Closing* sections of the sales process. During the early parts of the sales presentation, the sales person talks in a much more relaxed and natural tone of voice. Then when the sales person gives the Offer and the Close, he starts getting nervous because the prospect might give him an objection. He's going to ask the prospect for a commitment. He's going to ask the prospect for some money. And what happens? The sales person starts getting nervous and starts talking more quickly. The nervousness and tension creep into his voice and his body language, and the prospect picks it up *immediately*! You don't want prospects nervous, especially at the Close of the Sales Presentation!

Are you as effective in selling as a Girl Scout?

Let me ask you a question: *"Are you as effective in selling as a Girl Scout?"*

I'm not so sure.

Girl Scouts sell millions of dollars of cookies every year. Can you imagine having a part-time sales force that only works two months out of the year that sells millions of dollars in goods?

Here's why all the Girl Scouts are so successful selling millions of boxes of Girl Scout cookies every single year. Let's look at the <u>Offer and Closing</u> script first. Then we'll analyze it to show why it works.

The reason the Girl Scouts are so successful is they follow a script that is extremely powerful and includes the offer built right into it.

Here is the script: *"Hi, my name is Susie. Would you like to buy some boxes of delicious Girl Scout cookies?"* The offer is delivered naturally with a smile, and then the Girl Scout is silent. She has asked for the order and now is silent and waiting for the person to respond.

First of all, the Girl Scout is smiling to develop trust and rapport. Then she introduces herself. You now know her name. Then the offer: *"Would you like to buy some boxes of delicious Girl Scout cookies?"*

"Would you like to buy some boxes?" — she is asking for multiple purchases instead of just asking for the person to buy <u>one</u> box of Girl Scout cookies.

The word "delicious" links this to our need. We all love delicious food, especially cookies, and your stomach is a very powerful influencer of buying behavior. Have you ever gone grocery shopping when you're hungry?

You bought more food because your stomach was influencing your buying behavior.

After she asked for the order, she is silent! This gives the buyer time to make a decision. Too many salespeople talk themselves out of a sale because after asking for the order, they keep on talking.

Susie and the other Girl Scouts follow the script and remain silent after asking for the order. That's why the Girl Scouts are so successful!

Worksheet

This is both a textbook and a workbook. Grab a pen and on the following page write your offer. Remember to make your *Offer* as clear and concise as possible. People who take action are rewarded! Take your pen and write down your Offer.

Challenge yourself!

Offer

1. _____
2. _____
3. _____
4. _____
5. _____
6. _____
7. _____
8. _____
9. _____
10. _____
11. _____
12. _____
13. _____
14. _____
15. _____
16. _____
17. _____
18. _____

CHAPTER 6

Objections

"Objections": Excuses People Give You Not To Buy

Handling Objections

Sales professionals know how to **really** handle objections!

Let's talk about the common objections in your industry.

Here are some of the common objections salespeople often hear:

- Your price is too high.
- I need to think about it.
- I need more information.
- It's too complicated.
- What we already have is good enough.

Every industry has 7 to 12 common objections. Be sure to add the objections that are specific to your industry to your list of objections.

The goal for your sales team is to have 10 to 20 written responses **per objection** written down. Once again, every industry has around <u>7 to 12</u> common objections. This is good news. You can start developing responses to these common objections. There are *<u>3 ways</u>* to handle an objection:

1. Before it comes up,
2. After it comes up, or
3. Ignore it.

Before it comes up: The "<u>Mind-Reading</u>" Technique

How to use the Mind-Reading Technique:

The <u>Mind-Reading Technique</u> is a powerful way to bring up objections before they come up. Here's how it works. If salespeople were selling office copiers, this is how they could use the <u>Mind-Reading Technique</u>: *"You might be thinking to yourself, this new office copier looks complicated."* Now that the sales professional has raised the objection, he can answer in the most powerful way possible. If your salespeople handle any of the <u>7 to 12</u> common objections in the body of their presentation and finally get to the <u>Closing</u> section of the presentation and the prospect still gives a previous objection that was handled before, then you know the objection is a *<u>stall</u>* and not the real objection. This gives salespeople tremendous power and confidence in their presentations.

Watch Infomercials!

A great way to learn the <u>Mind-Reading Technique</u> is to watch *Infomercials*. In a 30-minute *Infomercial*, stories and other items are mentioned to handle the objection before it comes up. Many objections in *Infomercials* are handled with a story. The stories used in *Infomercials* are not accidental. Each story addresses a specific objection, so look at sales presentations and bring up the objections and then handle them in the body of your presentation. The salespeople will close more sales this way, and selling will be much more enjoyable. Plus, handling objections before they come up is an excellent technique for brand-new salespeople to use. Salespeople who are new to sales within your industry may not have heard many of the objections that they would get from a prospect.

After you have Closed

The traditional way to handle objections is to wait until you have closed, and the prospect gives you an objection. If you know the type of objections you hear, you can script <u>20 different responses</u> to each objection. When the prospect brings up the objection after you have closed, you can answer confidently and convincingly.

Remember to Pause

This is a problem that affects many experienced salespeople because they have heard almost all of the objections before, so these experienced salespeople have responses ready, and they respond almost instantly! The sales person must remember to pause before responding. The pause-of-silence demonstrates to the prospect that you're actively listening and also provides a much more natural rhythm of the flow of the conversation.

Ignore the objection.

Sometimes it is important to ignore the prospect's objection. This is especially true if you are presenting a _Front-of-the-Room_ group sales presentation.

What about an objection that is from left field?

"Really? I haven't heard that one before! Tell me more about it."

Learn 13 ways to handle objections.

<u>Story:</u>

Stories act as invisible selling. People are conditioned from a very young age to listen to stories. Stories are one of the most powerful ways to effectively sell people.

Top-producers and sales forces have a <u>Success Story Library</u>. Let me explain. Why are stories important in selling? For many reasons. As young children, our parents read to us stories. Stories kept us engaged, and we learned about the world through stories, so we are conditioned to listen to stories. Stories, when told, engage both sides of the brain: the analytical side (left brain) and the emotional side (right brain). When people hear stories, they tend to lower their resistance and might think to themselves: "The sales person is just telling me a story." But the story will make selling points.

Question

One of the most powerful ways to handle an objection is to question the objection. The language used to question the objection is as follows: *"Tell me more about that."* You need to really investigate the objection. Do not just accept it on face value. Think of it this way; You just delivered a well delivered sales presentation and shared all the benefits and reasons for them to take action. The prospect "owes you an explanation. You must use it to question the objection.

Solve the problem

You can find a way to solve the problem and thus solve the objection. Maybe the person is "too busy to meet with you." If you're meeting with doctors and dentists, they are extremely busy, running their practices, so agree to meet with them at times that are convenient for them, for example, 7 AM to 8:30 AM or after 5 PM. You can then agree to meet with them at times that are convenient for them. Thus you take away and solve the objection of their meeting with you. Think of ways for your own industry how you can solve objections.

One of my clients sells travel services. He met with a man who was claustrophobic and hated airplanes, so we solved the objection. He booked the man on a two-week exotic cruise and got him a limo ride from his house to the harbor! This is another example of how you can solve the problem and thus solve the objection.

Isolate

"Other than _____, is there anything else that's preventing you from moving forward today?"

Bring out the objection

This is another very simple, yet very powerful technique. Bringing out the objection is the opposite of isolating it. Oftentimes, the true objection is a non-stated objection. Many times the prospects will not reveal the true objection. Each objection that they give you is a *stall*, not an objection. When you use this technique, it encourages the prospect to be honest with you. Here is an example:

Objection: *"I don't have the money."*

Response: "I understand. So what you are saying is that you don't have the money. Is that correct?" (Repeated "yes" technique. Then ask a question and be silent.) Let them respond.

"I am sure that you have some other concerns before moving forward. Do you mind sharing those other concerns with me?" Let them respond.

Investigate

"Tell me more about that...."

Before it comes up

Once again, every industry has around 7 to 12 common objections. This is good news. You can start developing responses to these common objections. There are *3 ways* to handle an objection:

1. Before it comes up,
2. After it comes up, or
3. Ignore it

Share the Benefits

If you are getting a certain objection again and again, it may indicate that parts of your sales presentation need to be improved upon. Often sharing the benefits will handle the objection. For example, your system is easy to use and yet prospects are concerned about its being complicated. If you demonstrate how easy it is to use and get the prospect to practice using the system, then it makes the objection, "It's too complicated!" disappear. If you're getting common objections, take a look at your sales presentation and see if those objections could be made to go away by more effectively and clearly stating the benefits of your product or service.

Reduce the risk

Some people are afraid to buy because they are worried about making a mistake. There are many ways to reduce the risk of the person purchasing your product or service. Think about ways you can do this. A "no long-term commitment" is one tool to reduce the risk and to get prospects to take action. The prospect thinks to himself: If it doesn't work out, I'm not locked into anything. Another way to reduce the risk is using a guarantee or a product warranty. All of these tools help to reduce the risk. Be creative and look for ways to reduce the risk of the prospect buying your product or service.

Be unreasonable

One of the most powerful ways to handle an objection is to be unreasonable. Use this "be unreasonable" strategy when you have nothing left to lose. You use the "be unreasonable" objection-handling technique after you've handled many of the objections. If the person still comes back to the same objection which you handled in a different way previously, you can use the "be unreasonable" strategy.

Many years ago, I was in the financial services industry, selling financial products to high net-worth individuals. One of the common objections I got was, "I need to learn more about your company and your team prior to investing." I would handle that objection in several different ways; however, some people were still hesitant at this point. At this stage, I used the "be unreasonable" strategy to handle the objection. When the person would say, "I really need to meet the managers and the leaders of your company before I invest," I would handle the objection by being unreasonable:

"Then fly out here and see us! Our company is located in Orange County, right next to the John Wayne airport. You can fly out here with your wife and kids. Your wife and kids who can go to <u>Disneyland</u> for the day, and you can come meet the leaders of the company and the fund managers."

I had nothing more to lose when I handled the objection in this way. Ninety percent of the people who flew out to visit us bought!

Being unreasonable is a powerful technique that you can use to handle objections. Sales pros use this strategy when appropriate.

Negotiate

When you can negotiate, you often can handle the objection. By negotiating, you can change the terms of the deal and thus make the sale. You may have flexibility on pricing options or delivery dates or other ways to be flexible to win the deal. However, if you do not have pricing or other negotiation-flexibility, you must make your sales presentation as powerful and persuasive as possible to make the sale. One way to do this is to take away the *Offer* that is only good until 5 PM today! If you don't take advantage of it, the offer returns to the full price.

What would need to happen....

This script is a powerful way to get the person to tell you what needs to be done in order to handle the objection. For example, if you're selling a product to a manager who says that your offer is more than they can approve, *as is*. So ask them this question: *"What would need to happen to get this deal approved today?"* They will now tell you what the necessary steps are and what are some other ways to get the sale approved today. You then have them do that.

Objections

1. _____

2. _____

3. _____

4. _____

5. _____

6. _____

7. _____

8. _____

9. _____

10. _____

11. _____

12. _____

13. _____

14. _____

15. _____

16. _____

17. _____

18. _____

CHAPTER 7

Scripts You Need to Write

Spreadsheet

Prioritization *of Your* Scripts: **Urgency, Ease,** *or* **Value**

Top-Producing Sales People and Sales Forces know what *Scripts* they need to *Write*.

There are several different types of *Sales Scripts*:

- Main Presentation
- Appointment Setting
- Referrals
- Front-of-the-Room Scripts
- Conference Calls
- Objection Handling
- Follow-Up
- Recruiting
- Web Copy
- Sales Letters
- E-Mail's, and

- Voice Mail Scripts.

These are the scripts that you need to create for your business. You might be thinking to yourself: "That's a lot of scripts. Where do I start?" That brings us to our next tip: How to *prioritize* your list of scripts you need to get done.

How to Prioritize Your Script List

There are three ways to prioritize your scripts according to:

- Urgency
- Ease
- Value.

Urgency is a good way to prioritize which scripts you need to get done. If you have an appointment with a very important decision-maker at a large company next week, completing first your <u>Main Presentation Script</u> makes the most sense.

Ease: Sometimes people may feel a bit overwhelmed when writing their scripts, so they choose the easiest ones to do first, for example, they may complete their *Appointment Setting Script* first.

Value: The third way to prioritize your scripts is by *Value*. Using the following three worksheets will help you with this exercise.

Worksheet #1 (Blank)

Worksheets #2 and #3 are provided as examples.

Step #1

Look at <u>Worksheet #1</u> on the following page that lists the types of scripts that most businesses need. Next to each script on that list that applies to your business, write down the **dollar-value** to you by getting that particular script done over the next *12 months* in <u>Column #1</u>. It's okay to just estimate. Ask yourself this question: *"How much would having your Main Presentation Script finished mean to you over the next 12 months?"* Whatever dollar-figure comes to mind, write that down now. *"How much in dollars would it mean to you having your <u>Appointment Setting Script</u> done over the next 12 months?"* Whatever

Dollar-figure comes to mind right now, write that down. Do this for each one of your scripts on your list.

Step #2

Most people plan to be in professional selling for at least 10 years. Here's the next step. I want you to multiply your <u>12-month dollar figure</u> for each script (Column #1) by **10** and list your answers in Column #2. That gives you an idea of the lifetime-value of your getting your scripts completed, so prioritizing this list by **dollar-value** is very effective.

Step #3: For Sales Executives Only

Then multiply your 12 month figure for each script *by the number of sales people on your team* and write your answers in <u>Column #3</u>.

Prioritize Your Scripts to Complete in Descending Order

This powerful worksheet helps you to determine the **total dollar-value** of your team's getting its scripts completed. Whatever script has the highest value to you, complete that script first. Then complete the second highest value script.

In Worksheet Example #2, the scripts would be completed in the following order:

1. Main Presentation Script (Value $50,000)
2. Appointment Setting Script (Value $20,000)
3. Referral Script (Value $10,000).

Worksheet Example #1

	Script Type	Column #1 12-Month Value	Column #2 Lifetime (10-year value)	Column #3 X # of Salespeople
				1
1	Main Presentation	$	$	$
2	Appointment Setting	$	$	$
3	Referrals	$	$	$
4	Front-of-the-Room	$	$	$
5	Conference Call	$	$	$
6	Webinar	$	$	$
7	Objection Handling	$	$	$
8	Follow-up	$	$	$
9	Recruiting	$	$	$
10	Voicemail	$	$	$
11	In-Bound Calls	$	$	$
12	Walk-in	$	$	$
13	Email	$	$	$
14	Each Product Needs a Script	$	$	$
15		$	$	$
16		$	$	$
17		$	$	$
18		$	$	$
	Grand Total	$	$	$

Worksheet Example #2

	Script Type	Column #1 12-Month Value	Column #2 Lifetime (10-year value)	Column #3 X # of Salespeople
				1
1	Main Presentation	$50,000	$500,000	$500,000
2	Appointment Setting	$20,000	$200,000	$200,000
3	Referrals	$10,000	$100,000	$100,000
4	Front-of-the-Room	$	$	$
5	Conference Call	$	$	$
6	Webinar	$5,000	$50,000	$50,000
7	Objection Handling	$10,000	$100,000	$100,000
8	Follow-up	$	$	$
9	Recruiting	$5,000	$50,000	$50,000
10	Voicemail	$	$	$
11	In-Bound Calls	$	$	$
12	Walk-in	$	$	$
13	Email	$	$	$
14	Each Product Needs a Script	$	$	$
15		$	$	$
16		$	$	$
17		$	$	$
18		$	$	$
	Grand Total	$100,000	$1,000,000	$1,000,000

Worksheet Example #3

	Script Type	Column #1 12-Month Value	Column #2 Lifetime (10-year value)	Column #3 X # of Salespeople
				5
1	Main Presentation	$50,000	$500,000	$2,500,000
2	Appointment Setting	$20,000	$200,000	$1,000,000
3	Referrals	$10,000	$100,000	$500,000
4	Front-of-the-Room	$	$	$
5	Conference Call	$	$	$
6	Webinar	$5,000	$50,000	$250,000
7	Objection Handling	$10,000	$100,000	$500,000
8	Follow-up	$	$	$
9	Recruiting	$5,000	$50,000	$250,000
10	Voicemail	$	$	$
11	In-Bound Calls	$	$	$
12	Walk-in	$	$	$
13	Email	$	$	$
14	Each Product Needs a Script	$	$	$
15		$	$	$
16		$	$	$
17		$	$	$
18		$	$	$
	Grand Total	$100,000	$1,000,000	$5,000,000

CHAPTER 8

Appointment Setting Script

Are you in front-of a "<u>Qualified Buyer</u>?"

Appointment Setting Script

Appointment Setting Scripts are to get qualified prospects to meet with you about your product or service. The sole-purpose of an *Appointment Setting Script* is to get the prospect to meet with you. That's it!

Think of the graph below as a *see-saw* you would find at a children's playground. On the left hand side is "**Value**" and on the right side is "**Time.**"

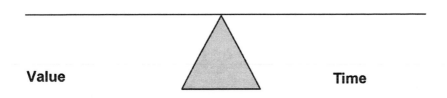

Value   **Time**

The Prospect is deciding, "How much value will I get with meeting you versus how much time I will spend?" What you want to do with your *Appointment Setting Script* is put as much weight on the "Value" side so it tips, and the prospect decides to set an appointment.

The **Appointment Setting Script** is one of the most important scripts to your long-term success. Complete it right away!

Appointment Setting Scripts: Value versus Time

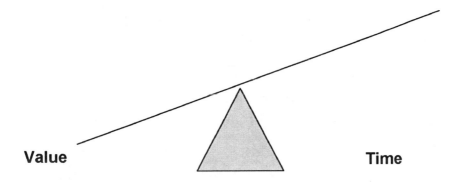

Appointment Setting Scripts: Stand-Alone Benefits

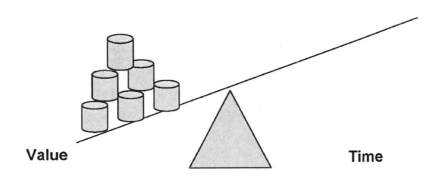

Hypnotic repetition is the key use of certain words or phrases over and over again throughout your presentation. You must remember to sprinkle these keywords or phrases throughout the presentation, so it does not come to the conscious awareness of your prospect. Don't be afraid to use this technique; it is one of the most powerful techniques you have available as a sales professional.

In the appointment setting script below, there are several keywords or phrases that are used hypnotically. Can you find them?

"Hi, my name is John, and I'm with this security company. I'm out talking to independent business owners who want to improve the productivity and profitability of their business operations. In this tough economy, crime is increasing, and new threats are quickly evolving. When we meet, you'll receive a customized crime report for your business address. This crime report focuses both on personal crime and property crime. Personal crime affects your safety and the safety of your employees. Property crime affects the physical safety of the business. When we meet, you will also learn some powerful ideas on ways to improve the profitability of your business.

CHAPTER 9

Main Presentation Script

"Are you as Powerful and Persuasive as Possible?"

Main Presentation Script:

The *Main Presentation Script* is when you are with a decision-maker who can make a buying decision. At the end of the *Main Presentation Script*, you will ask the person for a commitment to buy. If you don't ask for the order, it is not a *Main Presentation Script*!

A *Main Presentation Script* can be anywhere from 10 minutes to an hour or more in length. A good *Main Presentation Script* is long enough for the person to make a buying decision. Use the typical length of a *Main Presentation Script* in your industry as your guide.

Your <u>Main Presentation Script</u> has 5 steps:

1. Develop trust and rapport,
2. Identify customer needs and use of probing questions,

3. Share the benefits,
4. Offer, and
5. Objection Handling.

Step 1: Develop Trust and Rapport

What is trust and rapport? Let's define our terms because you often hear these words in the context of selling. What do these words really mean? **Trust**—*confidence in the integrity, ability, character, and truth of a person or thing.*

This *trust* definition describes a sales professional. They have confidence: confidence in themselves and in the products and services that they sell. If you do not feel 100% that your products and services or company are the best, it will negatively affect your selling and will affect your selling so much that you need to change jobs to find a product or service and company that you can 100% believe in!

Integrity—You do what you say and say what you do. This is the concept of under-promising and over-delivering. In sales, you must have total integrity, and you demonstrate your integrity or prospects by your actions. Sales professionals whose integrity and credibility in the eyes of your prospects by promising something and not following through.

Ability—People have trust in your ability. Trust in selling is developed through several areas:

• Your scripts,

- Your product knowledge, and
- Your process.

Your Scripts — A powerful way to develop trust! You use the most powerful and persuasive scripts and techniques. Your words are either drawing people closer to a sale or pushing them away. This entire book is about the power of *Scripts* to transform your selling.

Your product knowledge is important. It is necessary; however, it is not sufficient. If product knowledge were all that was required for customers to buy, they would just use a catalogue to make their purchase. People who shop at <u>Wal-Mart</u> do not need a salesperson to share with them the product-knowledge in order for them to make a buying decision. <u>Wal-Mart</u>'s customers have all the information they need to make a buying decision.

Be grateful that your salesperson. You must sell! But don't get caught in the "all I need is product knowledge" trap.

Your Proces — People must buy how you sell before they buy what you sell. Trust comes from your sales process. Potential clients are secretly begging for a quality sales presentation. A salesperson guides the potential customer with a clear step-by-step process will develop trust.

A 42-Point Inspection

I bought my wife a beautiful pre-owned Honda from the local dealership. The car was put through a 42-Point

Inspection before it was made available for sale. I know they check the brakes, oil, the engine, and the air-conditioning. I don't need to know what other 35 items that they checked. Just knowing that they checked those points gave me more confidence in my buying decision. I could have read every single item that they checked in that 42- Point Inspection; however, that they had put the car through that process was enough to help me feel more confidence in making a buying decision.

Character is more of who you are. Are all your actions and words truthful? This is essential for your long-term sales success.

CHAPTER 10

Extended Sales Cycle

"From a few weeks to a few months"

"Group Decisions"

The key to *Sales Scripting* in an extended sales cycle is:

- Who
- What
- When
- How, and
- Why

This will allow you to map your extended sales cycle and extended sales process. An *Extended Sales Process* is sometimes called a <u>Complex Sale</u>.

Who

"Who" in this case involves multiple people. You must identify the "who" at each stage of the *Extended Sales Cycle*. Note that each company is unique, and there are patterns. Focus on the various people you meet within an *Extended Sales Cycle* for your industry.

Once you know your "Who", you can *Script* accordingly. A Middle-manager has different needs and different benefits than an Executive Vice-president or CEO. You must know and script how to talk to each of them; furthermore, you may be presenting to a decision-committee, so you must be able to blend the *Script* where appropriate.

What

What do they want? What are their hot-buttons? Where is their pain? You must structure your presentation with benefit language that will resonate with each person you are presenting to.

When

When do they need it? When is an acceptable delivery date? Everyone in an organization will say: "We want it tomorrow." It's important to find out their expectations. You need to manage their expectations now and during the implementation phase. Failure to manage expectations often leads to frustration and disappointment with the person or organization you are dealing with.

How

How you sell in a *complex sale* is just as important as

what you sell. What is your sales process? Can you articulate to the client how the process works? Of course, you need to be flexible, and you must keep in mind how each person likes to be sold to.

Why

Why do they want to do it? What is their *benefit-of-the-benefit*?

The *Extended Sales Cycle* requires a roadmap with key milestones to complete. Each milestone in the process will require a different approach and different *Scripts*. Who is present at each milestone also has a big impact on the sale.

You need to remember that the outcome for each milestone is to be able to move on the next step of the *Extended Sales Cycle*. Which stage you are in will affect what types of *Sales Scripts* you write.

A typical buying process goes through the following stages:

1. Recognition of Needs
2. Evaluation of Options
3. Resolution of Concerns,
4. The Buying Decision, and
5. Implementation.

These 5 steps are a simple buying process.

The number of steps in this process could go out for

weeks or months, depending on what you're selling. If you are selling jumbo jets, the *Extended Sales Cycle* can take years. Take the above 5 steps as a starting model and adapt them to your business.

Recognition of Needs

In this step, the buyers understand that they have a problem and define a range of solutions. It is critical for you to help them understand and articulate their problems. At this time, they may have a gut-feeling that something is wrong. This is more a feeling of *unease*. It is essential to help the prospective buyers to really articulate their pain.

At this stage, the buyer defines a range of possible solutions. It is important for you to help guide this conversation on defining what the range of solutions is, and you want to do this in such a way that presents your firm is the best choice.

How do you do this? One way is with a **Free Report**. What is in your free report helps them to define the range of solutions that also impacts the next step in the *Evaluations of Options* where the buyer determines the decision criteria.

Resolutions of Concerns

The buyer identifies and resolves the perceived risks with the Sales Professional and sometimes resolves the perceived risks after the meeting with the Sales Professional is over.

The Buying Decision

The person or a committee makes the buying decision.

Implementation

The key here is to mange expectations, so the customer remains happy, and you can receive repeat business and referrals.

CHAPTER 11

Mirroring

"The Power of the Sword, the Jewel, and the Mirror"

There is a <u>Zen</u> story. A Zen Master asks his three students: *"What is the most powerful, the Sword, the Jewel, or the Mirror?"*

The first student answers: *"The power of the sword. The sword is most powerful because with it you are strong and can take what you want or defend yourself."*

The Master replies: *"Incorrect."*

The second student answers: *"The Jewel is the most powerful because you can buy what you want and can influence many people."*

The Master states: *"Incorrect."*

The third student answers: *"The Mirror is the most powerful. The mirror promotes reflection. Seek and reflect on yourself and improve yourself."*

The Master confirms: *"You are correct."*

The power of the mirror is appropriate for selling. You need to use tools to reflect upon your performance and look for areas of improvement. Using a digital recorder to record your *Script* and look for ways to improve your *Scripts* is extremely powerful. Tracking your ratios and track your performance from day-to-day, week-to-week, and month-to- month are other important tools.

The power of the mirror also applies to mirroring other people.

Pace, Pace, Pace, and Lead

You must pace your prospect while leading them towards the sale. This is the fundamental rhythm of the sales presentation: pace, pace, pace, and lead. You have three pacing statements followed by a leading statement. The prospects do not feel rushed, and you are still guiding them towards making a sale.

Here's an example from automotive sales. The prospect has walked into the showroom and has looked at two of the same models of vehicles but in different colors.

Sales professional: *"I notice you're looking at the Honda Civic models on our show room floor. [Pace] You looked at the red one and the silver one. [Pace] You also paid close attention to the miles per gallon information on the car window. [Pace] Let me answer your questions before we take it for a test drive." [Leading statement]*

Mirroring: Synchronize Breathing

By *synchronizing breathing* with your prospect is a powerful way to develop trust and rapport. *Synchronizing breathing* is virtually invisible to the conscious mind.

Mirroring: Synchronize Posture and Body Movement

This is another tool for effectively developing *trust and rapport*. You are <u>mirroring and matching</u> the prospects' posture and body movement. Note, you're not imitating them! Synchronizing posture is very easy to do. You want to mirror subtly, for example, but do not try to mirror nervous tics that a person has.

Mirroring: Synchronize Voices

Synchronizing voices involves mirroring voice rate, volume, and pitch. This is a powerful tool to effectively build *trust and rapport*, even in sales over the telephone, and if you just mirror voices, you'll be ahead of 80% of your competition will not do this.

Mirroring: Synchronize with Your Target

<u>Mirroring</u> your target deepens trust and rapport that must be an essential part of your selling strategy.

CHAPTER 12

VAK's Level of Scripting

"Do You Think with Your Eyes, Ears, Fingers, Nose, or Stomach?"

Scientists have determined that there are five ways that people process information. These five ways of processing information or ways of thinking are based on the five primary senses:

- Visual (eyes)
- Auditory (ears)
- Kinesthetic (touch)
- Gustatory (taste), and
- Olfactory (smell).

People have one dominant thinking style. You can determine their thinking style by their language! You can determine a person's dominant thinking style by the language patterns or language predicates they use when they talk.

Why is this useful in selling? Visual people like data.

My main thinking style is more visual. I love to see things, charts, graphs, and data. Originally, I was more successful selling to engineers, people who tend to be more analytical. I was losing sales because I was not presenting the proper styles that could be absorbed and acted upon. It was frustrating for them and frustrating for me until I learned the *dominant thinking styles* and then as I started to include them into my sales presentation, my skills improved.

Determine How They Represent Information (The VAK's)

There are three dominant thinking styles: *Visual, Auditory,* and *Kinesthetic.* When you are presenting to groups, make sure you focus on all three thinking styles for your message to be received by all three groups; otherwise, you'll be alienating the people who don't reflect your thinking style in your audience. In an individual sales presentation, you must make sure that you focus on these three points while determining the dominant thinking style of your prospect. Once you determine the *dominant thinking style* of your prospect, you can then tailor the rest of your presentation to their particular thinking style, and you'll develop much greater trust and rapport.

3 Thinking Styles

- Visual
- Auditory
- Kinesthetic

Include word examples for each type of thinking style in your speech; therefore, you will more effectively reach each member of your audience.

Fortunately, there are *three dominant thinking styles*, so you can weave them into your presentation, so the various language predicates reach their preferred way of communicating and receiving information. These are based on the *language predicates*. See the list below. Examples of **Visual** words or phrases to use in your speech:

Analyze	Survey	Inspect	Examined	Look over
Beautiful	Attractive	Handsome	Good-looking	Gorgeous
Beautiful	Attractive	Handsome	Good-looking	Gorgeous
Pretty	Stunning	Elegant	Clear	Plain
Focus	Look	Look at	Watch	Picture
Visualize	See in your mind's eye	Take a look at		

Examples of **audio** words and phrases to use in your speeches:

Announce	Made public	Report	Declare	Notify	
Broadcast	Talk over	Debate	Talk about	Express	
Communicate	Put into words	Hear	Listen to		
Inquire	Ask	Noise	Din	Clamor	Racket
Proclaim	Roar	yell	Cry	Howl	Boom
Crash	Thundering	Say	Speak	Shout	

Scream	Silence	Quiet	Muffle	Tell
Report	Voice	Express		

Examples of **kinesthetic,** or **action** words and phrases to use in your speech:

Active	Attack	Energetic	Mobile	Beat up
Charge	Cool	Chill	Cold	Deep
Bottomless	Embrace	Hug	Grasp	Hold
Squeeze	Solid	Dense	Hot	Steamy
Motion	Movement	Shifting	Rough	Bumpy
Rocky	Shock	Smooth	Flat	Soft

One of my clients, named Mark, sells custom-built estate homes to the wealthy. Each home cost between $5 and $25 million. He has taken his main presentation script and written one for visual, auditory, and kinesthetic types of thinkers. When he knows what the person's *dominant thinking style* is, he will then pivot into that particular script for that particular thinking style. Because he is selling a $5 and $25 million product, it's to Mark's advantage to be as powerful and persuasive as possible. Don't leave anything to chance! Think about your highest-end product or service, the one you charge the most for. I challenge you to create three separate scripts based on the visual, auditory, and kinesthetic. Then you can pivot to which one is the most appropriate in that particular selling situation.

What about selling to couples or committees? You will cycle through all the free-thinking styles in your presentation and when you are in the *question-and-answer* period, and then you can answer questions according to that person's individual thinking style which will be more powerful and more persuasive.

CHAPTER 13

Selling One-on-One

"The Dynamics of one-to-one Selling"

This chapter is titled the <u>Dynamics of One-to-One Selling</u> because it is a collaborative process. What are the dynamics that you need to focus on? We have already covered some of the group-selling dynamics in the chapter, "The Extended Sales Cycle." Now we will focus on the 1 to 1 dynamics.

First of all, you must be dynamic! Regardless of how proficient you have become with your scripts, you cannot be simply going through the motions. If you are "bored" with your presentation or it is on auto-pilot, you have a big problem. The potential client can feel boredom or apathy just as easily as excitement and enthusiasm!

You Must Be Present

You must be *Present* with the prospect. What does being *Present* look like? Being *Present* involves:

- Physiology,
- Action,
- Mindset, and
- the Selling Environment.

Physiology

Physiology is essential to being present. Are you leaning forward? Do you mentally notice their eye color? Mentally noting their eye color is one powerful way to develop trust and rapport and to be *Present*. If you are standing, what is your stance? Are you mirroring their physiology? Using your physiology properly is a powerful way to be Present with potential customers, and they will feel <u>heard</u>.

Actions

How are you listening? Are you really actively listening? Many sales people are not very good listeners. Remember, you have two ears and one mouth for a reason. Actively listening means you are hanging on their every word is a way to develop the *presence* that is required. Paraphrasing and summarizing their statements to demonstrate that you have heard them is also very important. Are your actions consistent and congruent? Do you use your hands properly with your gestures? Some people gesticulate wildly with their hands and thus the gestures lose their effectiveness.

Mindset

What is your mindset? Are you expecting to make the sale going in? What are your outcomes for the sale? Your first outcome would be to make the sale. The secondary outcome would be to get referrals. Your mindset determines whether you are dynamic and present or mentally absent. Is your mindset coming from a place of service, namely, that you view selling as a service?

Believe it or not, some sales people have the antiquated mindset that "the prospect has my money in his pocket, and it's my job to get it."

Environment

You control more of your selling environment than you might think. Location: at your office, at their home, or at a neutral location. You need to find which environment positively influences your selling dynamic the most. It may be your office. Maybe your office is in a prestigious location, and this positively impacts your relationship with your potential customers or clients; in addition, you can block out distractions and can spend more time with potential customers because you do not have to commute.

At the customers home or office

Often, when you visit potential customers at their home or office, the clients will be more relaxed because they are in a familiar environment. They are on their "home turf," if you will. The customers might listen more and be more attentive in this type of environment, and their resistance might be lower.

Neutral 3rd Party Location

This is very important for 1 to 1 interpersonal dynamics. You could meet at a coffee shop. This could be a convenience-factor that influences the interpersonal 1 to 1 dynamics. In high-level negotiations, a neutral third party location facilitates the process because neither side has a location-advantage. A neutral location also facilitates dialogue, so you may have to start a discussion with a potential strategic alliance partner at a local coffee shop.

The situation where you go to the potential clients home or office or meet at neutral location, you have a lot more control than you might think. At the person's home, you can suggest you sit at the kitchen table. More business is done at the home around the kitchen table than anywhere else. This is a powerful way to influence one-on-one dynamics. Ask them to turn off the TV or radio, so they can focus on your conversation. Turn your own cell phone to OFF or SILENT. Even a vibrating cell phone will cause a distraction and will negatively affect the one-on-one dynamic.

If you are meeting at a neutral location, recommend a place that is relatively quiet. A coffee shop might not be the best location.

What about all this talk about being present?

Definition of Presence — a person's manner of carrying himself, the quality of self-assurance and confidence.

What are some other ways one can develop *Presence*?

1. Authenticity
2. Congruency
3. Relevancy

Authenticity

You must be true to yourself. It is also a belief in your product or service. Without a belief in your product or service, you will not make sales because the prospect can tell the lack of conviction in your product.

Congruency

Do your actions match your words and your words match your actions? Any discrepancies and the potential customers will feel it. They may not be consciously aware of it, but they will feel it. Anything that feels incongruent affects the one-to-one dynamics.

Relevancy

Is what you are saying to the potential clients relevant to their situation? If your content is not relevant to their needs, then you are not relevant either. It is up to you to script your presentation and deliver it, so the potential customers feel it is relevant. That responsibility is up to you.

Two Stories about Presence

When I was overseas working and living in Taiwan, I was a member of a <u>Toastmasters Club</u>. One of our club members was a retired 3-star general from the Taiwan air force. He had been retired for several years before he joined our club. The club was made up of civilians, but he was not an elected club officer; nevertheless, he still had the *command presence*. In club interactions, you just sensed that he was accustomed to leading and acted accordingly.

Another club member was a Taiwanese Opera singer. In one-on-one interactions and when she spoke, she had the *presence* of a performer.

What is important from these stories is to find your own *selling presence* and embrace it. This will positively impact your selling.

CHAPTER 14

"Are Your Scripts Customized for Your Industry and Personalized for Your Unique Selling Style?"

Customized for Your Industry

This is not a conversation about *Jargon*. This is a conversation about establishing *Credibility*. The credibility comes through your use of language. The clearer you are, the better the results you will get. What is important is the tone of your Script. Is the Script consistent with the tone of your industry? For example, in financial services, you would never say: *"We have fun with your money."* The tone is all wrong! The tonality of the words must be consistent with your industry; on the other hand, the tone for a sales presentation for cruises would not have the tone of a life insurance presentation!

Now, having the right "tone" for your presentation does not mean it has to be boring! Southwest Airlines talks about how their flights are consistently on-time and that they have low fares and yet their passengers have a lot of fun, so you can make your presentation consistent with the "tone" of your industry and not have a boring or uninteresting one.

Current Scripts

Remember *Scripts* are living documents. The scripts must be updated regularly; otherwise, you have a script that worked many years before, but the market and selling environment has changed, so your script must be current and relevant. As a sales manager, you should review the sales scripts twice a year by testing them yourself and going on ride-along's with your salespeople at various skill levels throughout your organization.

Unfortunately, I see in companies, scripts that were working a few years ago but are no longer current. This is costing the company sales and increasing the turnover rate of sales people. One of the biggest offenders in using outdated scripts is in the financial services industry. This is because of having to put many scripts through the Compliance Department. For many financial services companies, the Compliance Department is run by lawyers who make sure the scripting language is fully compliant with the Security and Exchange Commission rules and regulations. Some of these scripts are years out of date! They sound antiquated when you listen to them, yet the scripts are not being updated because the sales manager feels that running the scripts by the Compliance Department is too much of a hassle. The responsibility of a high-level sales manager is to give salespeople the tools to help them succeed. If it takes some time to get a current and more persuasive script approved by the company's Compliance Department, then so be it.

Personalization for Your Unique Selling Style

Some companies do offer *Sales Scripts* to their salespeople. This is an excellent starting point! For maximum power and persuasiveness, your scripts must fit your unique selling style; otherwise, the scripts do not feel congruent nor authentic to the sales person; as a result, they wing-it. And when you wing-it, you get wing-it results.

Here is an example of a closing technique.

You may have heard about the "Alternative of Choice" *Close*. This is where you give the person two choices to purchase. Either option he chooses is a *yes*. Many sales people use the "Alternative of Choice" *Close* because it is so effective.

Some of the sales people I have worked with felt the "Alternative of Choice" *Close* was "too pushy." And yet they must ask a closing question. In this case, if the person does not like to feel congruent with the "Alternative of Choice" Close, he will not use it and be back to winging-it.

So it is important that the sales person can ask a closing question that is personalized to his unique selling style, so he could ask this closing question instead: "*How do you feel about moving forward today?*"

CHAPTER 15

Selling to Groups
Front-of-the-Room Scripts

"High Leverage Selling"

Front-of-the-Room Scripts

Front-of-the-Room Scripts are one-to-many selling situations. There are many Front-of-the-Room selling situations. The following are typical:

- An in-home party like a Tupperware party
- A Financial Planner hosting a dinner workshop
- A public speaker delivering an all-day seminar to hundreds of people

Front-of-the-Room Scripts are high-leverage selling.

For example, a typical face-to-face presentation takes one hour.

Now, imagine you are selling to 20 people in a Front-of-the-Room setting for just one hour.

You are conducting 20 presentations in just one hour, and that's why Front-of-the-Room scripts are powerful and high-leverage selling.

Think about how you can deliver a Front-of-the-Room selling script for your business.

If you are speaking in the front-of-the-room, you'll need to establish trust and rapport with your audience. Even though you are the expert and are on the stage speaking to the group, you need to seem approachable and just like everybody else. One way to do this is delivering your "mess to success" story. The mess-section is where the person was struggling and was not very successful. The mess section could be a few months or even a few years. What this does is establish in the audience's mind that you are like everybody else and can relate to you. The "success" section is what turned her life around. The mess to success scripting technique is best used in the front of the room speaking situation; however, not every speaker needs to use it, but a speaker should tell this story to gain credibility to a larger audience.

Interest Creating Remarks [ICR's] make for strong and interesting speeches, so use them throughout your speech to keep the audience's attention. ICR's are important to hold and keep your audience's attention because sometimes the individual's attention begins to drift, and if you are not careful, their attention may never return to your speech. To avoid that situation, use ICR's to redirect and keep the audience's attention. Here are a few examples of ICR's.

"The following is a real golden nugget that can help you in your career."

"Listen up. I'm about to share with you the 3 biggest mistakes people make when writing a résumé and how to avoid them."

There are 7 secrets to successful job interviews that few job seekers know. Knowledge of these secrets could be the difference between getting a great job offer and having to spend weeks or months job searching.

- Secret #1 is....
- Secret #2 is....
- Secret #3 is....

The 30-second elevator script is one of the most important scripts that you will create. This is used in many networking events. Sometimes the 30–second elevator script is called your "30–second commercial," which is a bit misleading. Beverage companies like Pepsi can spend millions of dollars on 30–second commercials to build their "brand." As a business owner or sales professional, your 30-second elevator script is designed to produce a qualified lead! That's it. You get a qualified lead to talk to about your product or service.

Sometimes when networking in Chambers of Commerce you are asked to stand up and give your 30-second elevator script.

Mistakes to Avoid

The first mistake is starting off with your name or your company's name. At this moment, the audience members are getting used to the sound of your voice. If there is any background noise, they may not hear your name at all.

The second mistake is not using benefit-language in your 30-second elevator script. Explain a few of the powerful benefits of your product or service. People buy benefits so what's in it for them? How will they benefit if they buy your product or service? You must speak in benefit language in your script.

Mistake number three is focusing on the how or the features. At a networking event a person from a nutritional and wellness company was talking about "you get the three proteins shakes a day." The audience members don't care about this at this point. What they care about is can they lose weight, get better nutrition, have more energy, and enjoy better health? That is what they really want. The three vitamin shakes is just a way to achieve that.

Mistake number four is not building group rapport. Even though you're in a group setting, you can build trust and rapport quickly and easily. We all like to do business with people we know, like, and trust. Many people forget this in their elevator scripts.

Mistake number five is focusing on your title. In your

elevator script focusing on your title; for example, "I'm a vice president, president or CEO of my company" is a big mistake. Your title acts as a barrier for people to talk with you. The title introduces hierarchy between you and the other person, and it states that you and the other person are not equals. You want people to talk with you and not push them away!

Mistake number six is no call-to-action. Tell what you want them to do. They cannot read your mind! So many people in their elevator scripts have no called-to-action, and they wonder why no one talks to them.

A networking group that is in Southern California is called the *Relationship Building Network* (RBN). It is a dynamic organization with 8,200 attendees each week. There is the 30-second elevator script, and people who are interested are asked to fill out a Lead-capture Form or *Green Card* to write down the person's name or RBN number to whom they want to speak. I will share with you my 30-second elevator script and then analyze it line by line.

"Fellow RBN members and honored guests. In this economy, it is more important than ever before to win customers because customers are the lifeblood of your business. When you become better at selling, you will win more customers, make more money, and grow your business. The sooner you talk to me, the more customers you will win. The longer you wait the more customers you will lose. To learn how you can win more customers, grab your pen and write down my name on a green card. My name is John, and my RBN number is 391."

Let's analyze the script line-by-line. "Fellow RBN members and honored guests." The audience gets accustomed to the sound of my voice, and it's a script for developing trust and rapport with the group. I acknowledge my fellow RBN members, so we have that bond in common, and I remind them of that fact. I also mentioned the honored guests. I have now included everyone in the room and quickly develop trust and rapport with them.

"In this economy, it is more important than ever before to win customers because customers are the lifeblood of your business." This is an advanced scripting technique called *"an undeniable truth." An undeniable truth* is a statement that everyone can agree with. What it does is people agree with you and start nodding their heads. What happens in the person's mind is this: "John is talking sense. I'll keep listening to what he has to say."

Also note the benefit: "To win more customers." That's a benefit that people want. This is the ultimate benefit. The *how* is not so important this time because it is a 30-second elevator script.

"When you become better at selling, you will win more customers, make more money, and grow your business." I mentioned how to become better at selling only briefly and then mention the benefits to win more customers, make more money, and grow your business.

I use another advanced scripting technique by the *benefits of taking action* and *the consequences of not taking action*. People are motivated by two things: getting into pleasure and avoiding pain. Both of these techniques are designed to motivate people to take action and to talk to me. The sooner you will talk to me the more customers you will win. The longer you wait the more customers you will lose.

The call to action

"To learn how you can win more customers, grab your pen and write down my name on a green card. My name is John, and my RBN number is 391." This script produces quality leads, week-after-week.

CHAPTER 16

Sales Presentation Analysis: A Step-by-Step Guide

The Sales Presentation Analysis is extremely powerful after you have written-out your baseline *Main Presentation Script*. After implementing the *Sales Scripting Strategies and Techniques* found in this book, your scripts will be more powerful and persuasive. The *Sales Presentation Analysis* is the next step.

The *Sales Presentation Analysis* can be used with new or seasoned sales people; this exercise can be used to make sure the Sales Scripting Main Presentation is current. Analyzing your *Main Presentation Script* should be done annually, or at a minimum, once every two years.

Here's how the process works. List all of the reasons or sales arguments that you use in your sales presentation that would get the customer to buy from you. I recommend doing the Sa*les Presentation Analysis* with a spreadsheet.

The next step: Evaluate how strong the sales argument is! On a scale of 1 to 10, 1 is a weak argument and a 10 is an argument that gets the person to buy immediately! A 9 is a decisive selling point. An 8 or a 7 is important. A 6 is a point barely worth mentioning. Sales points ranked from 1-5 are unimportant to meaningless. Sales points ranked 1-5 have no place in your presentation. If there are sales points ranked 1-5 in your presentation, they are making your presentation too long and add no value. Remove them immediately!

Next Step: Evaluate your Sales Points from Your Customer's Point of View

What are all the reasons for buying your product or service from the customer's point of view? Many sales people have never even asked themselves this question. What are all the buying reasons from your customer's point of view? Rank them on a 1-10 point scale. How does the customer view your sales points? Make sure the sales points that are included in your Main Presentation script the customer also values highly.

Next Point: Compensating Arguments to Handle Objections

Your product or service has disadvantages from the customer's point-of-view. EVERY product or service has disadvantages from the customer's point-of-view. You must address these objections, either raising them your-self (using the mind-reading technique) or after you have closed and the prospect brings it up.

CHAPTER 17

"How Do You Handle the Ups?"

Avoid *Jargon*!

Define your terms, so you and your audience are all on the same page. Jargon can be described as *industry* terms that only insiders would know. For people in the industry, jargon actually speeds up communication, but in a speech, jargon can be deadly! Jargon acts as a barrier between you and your audience.

If the members of the audience do not understand the term that you use, they will feel confused, embarrassed, or even angry, and an angry audience is not what you want!

If you are going to introduce a new term to your audience, use the following script: *"What I mean by that is…."*

When can you use *Jargon*?

There is a time and place to use jargon, but it must be used very carefully and used when you are extremely confident that it will work. Jargon can be used to establish instant rapport and instant credibility. Now, if you're going to use jargon, you have to know exactly what it means. If you use jargon like "name dropping", it will backfire on you!

Let me share a story. I was at a networking meeting, and there was a sales manager from a local Lexus dealership. In the car industry, a potential customer who walks onto the car lot is called an "up." At some dealerships, the first salesperson who sees a potential customer walk onto the lot gets the opportunity to sell him a car. In these types of dealerships, it is advantageous to be tall like an NBA basketball player, so you can see the "ups" first!

In other dealerships, there are other systems for allocating potential customers to the salespeople. Every dealership is different.

Since I knew I was talking to a sales manager at a Lexus dealership and had a lot of knowledge about the industry, I used *jargon* strategically. I asked the sales manager: *"How do you handle the ups?"* This script developed instant credibility and incident rapport with the sales manager.

Define Your Terms

Defining your terms is essential to successful communication. *Jargon*, or industry-terminology, often creeps into sales presentations which ultimately confuses the prospect. Prospects who are embarrassed and don't know something rarely buy. First, you should avoid industry jargon whenever possible. If you have to use the term, be sure you define it with the prospect, so both of you are on the same page throughout the presentation. Something as common as a 401(k) needs to be described and defined; otherwise, you and the prospect will be having two different "conversations" about what a 401(k) means.

CHAPTER 18

Image and Congruency
"Consistency: Inside and Outside"

Image, Congruency, Consistency, and Authenticity

Image

Product packaging makes a huge difference in the perceived value of a product. That is why so much attention is paid to getting the product packaging right so you must be dressed appropriately for your target market. Note, you can be overdressed for your target market! Let me explain.

Years ago, I was selling burglar alarms and camera systems to small business owners. These are mom-and-pop businesses with 5 to 25 employees. Part of my prospecting strategy was to "door knock" and walk to the store and speak with the owner. I was wearing a suit and tie. Frankly, I was overdressed for my target market that impacted my selling. A more appropriate outfit would have been khaki pants and a well-made polo shirt. That would've been the appropriate dress.

Consistency

Consistency is another way to build trust. Consistency over time is what makes a brand so successful. You know instantly what the brand is. Consistency in selling deals with your image and congruency. If you are random, you'll be perceived as incongruent and inconsistent. Do what you say and say what you'll do is another maximum in selling. Why? The underlying focus here is on consistency. That is why using the scripts to help you close sale after sale will make you more persuasive and more consistent.

Authenticity

You have the right image, you are congruent, and you are consistent; then you achieve authenticity. Being authentic is true and real to yourself and your customers. Being authentic is the point of power in selling!

Make Body and Words Say the Same Thing

Congruency is essential to successful selling! By congruent I mean that everything is in alignment and is consistent. If there is a mismatch between your body language and the words that you say, the prospect will pick this up subconsciously and begin to worry. This is another reason why you must dress professionally when meeting a prospect. You would never try to sell a CEO in shorts and a T-shirt because this would be incongruent.

CHAPTER 19

Duplicating Your Top Producers: How to Transform your Sales People into a Sales Force

Duplicating your top producers can be done both from a scripting point of view and from a sales manager's perspective. In *Scripting*, we've talked about modeling your top producers, regarding the scripts they use and crafting the strongest sales presentation possible, using the techniques found in this book.

Hiring Sales People

There are many benefits and advantages for finding and recruiting sales superstars:

- Benefits to you
- Competitive Advantages, and
- Benefits to your Sales Force.

Benefits to You, the Sales Executive

<u>Recruiting</u>: By recruiting top sales professionals,

you will have all the people you need to expand your business. You will have a SYSTEM in place that finds the hidden talent your competitors overlook. Also, since you have an on-going system in place, you will have a reservoir of top-candidates in place to fill any unexpected vacancies and to capitalize on business opportunities that will bring continuity and stability to your business.

Competitive Advantage

A fully staffed sales office is not just a collection of salespeople; it is a Sales Force! Long-term competitive advantages accrue to Sales Executives who have a system in place that constantly provides superior candidates to fill any job-openings, so you are never rushed into quickly hiring someone.

Your competitors are lurching from hire to hire because they don't know where and how to find top talent. They have no system in place and frequently choose a bad hire. Your competitors' offices are beset by high turnover of sales people that leads to customer dissatisfaction, customer defections, and many "orphan" accounts. They do not have the time to fully train their sales people!

That is *their* problem!

You know better!

Benefits to Your Sales Force

When you follow the system and are recruiting high quality sales professionals to your team, many good things happen. Your new hires **strengthen** your overall sales force because they want to be part of a winning team and will work hard and act accordingly. Your veteran salespeople see that you are enhancing the overall effectiveness of the sales force. You are NOT diluting the sales force with marginal hires. What you are creating is a community of like-minded professionals.

Recruiting Must Be an On-Going Process

That is why it's so important to have a **system**. If your recruiting methods are reactive and improvised, you will make a rushed decision that usually results in a poor fit for the position and leads to a bad hire!

The Recruiting Cycle goes through 9 Steps:

- Step 1: Profiles of Ideal Candidates with and without previous sales experience
- Step 2: Online and Offline Lead Sources
- Step 3: Initial Contact and Pre-Qualify
- Step 4: Business Briefing Group Presentation
- Step 5: Interview #1
- Step 6: Interview #2
- Step 7: Position(s) filled and other qualified candidates put into the Reservoir
- Step 8: Evaluate your recruiting ratios

- Step 9: Lessons Learned and update your recruiting profile

There is more to this process than can be covered in this chapter; however, this is a model you can follow to recruit all the qualified sales people you need.

Identify Excellence. Whom are you Really looking for?

Step #1:

Webster's Dictionary defines the word composite as: *"adj. 1. made up of disparate or separate parts or elements; compound."*

Without a clear picture of your ideal candidate-profiles, you will be stumbling around in the dark. "I'll know a good candidate when I see one" is just an excuse, so you need to create profiles of ideal candidates. The profiles fall into two categories:

- Candidates with previous sales experience, and
- Candidates without previous sales experience.

Your profile is really a composite of what skills, characteristics, and behaviors are necessary for success.

Include the job description for the sales person and know who your target customers are. Define them. Then ask yourself: "What type of Sales Professional would best be able to sell and serve these types of accounts?" Try to limit your job description to one page. A two-page job description is the maximum length. After you write the job *description, then have someone in* <u>*Human Resources*</u> *(HR) or the Legal Department* make sure your written job description is fully compliant with the law; however, do not abdicate responsibility of writing the job description to them.

Profiles of Candidates with Previous Sales Experience

Use a composite of the top-producers in your office. Look at the various professional skills and character traits necessary to succeed in the position. Create a list of "Must have's" and "Nice-to-have's." This is your first profile to help you find quality candidates with previous sales experience.

Candidate Profiles without Previous Sales Experience

There are some "diamonds in the rough" that you don't want to accidentally overlook. Look for *transferrable* skills. Look for leadership potential and look for character. Look for being coachable. Create a list of "Must have's" and "Nice-to-have's." Now with the candidates without previous sales experience, you must make absolutely sure your training system can get them up to speed quickly on the selling part of the job; otherwise, you are doing them and yourself a disservice.

You now KNOW whom you are looking for!

How Much Time is spent selling?

How much of your salesperson's time is spent actually selling? Many salespeople spend too much time on administrative tasks and not enough time in front of qualified prospects so look at your time-logs. Look for ways to reduce or eliminate non-sales tasks and have them spend more time selling. True salespeople prefer to sell anyway, so why not give them what they want?

Territory Management

Are your territories the right size? If the territories are too small, the salesperson cannot make a decent living and will eventually leave. This turnover of salespeople is expensive in dollars spent in training and impaired relationships with customers. On the other hand, if the territory is too big, that is also problematic. In this situation, there are too many customers for that salesperson to handle. Business is being lost because existing accounts cannot be serviced, and new business is not getting the attention it deserves.

Non-Monetary Motivation

Your top-producing salespeople are hitting their numbers and making good money, so what else can motivate them? You must find out from each one of them individually. Maybe the non-monetary motivation is greater recognition the top-producer is looking for. Maybe it's the opportunity to mentor a new sales person. Find that information out and use it.

You also must recognize and work with your top-producers while not ignoring your other sales staff. It is a fine line to walk, but it must be done.

CHAPTER 20

Layers of Scripting

"How Many Layers on the Wedding Cake?"

After mastering these various techniques, you can layer several scripting techniques in one sentence. Layering the scripts gives a cumulative effect that is more powerful than each technique used separately. When you're able to create layered scripts and deliver them effectively, you are on your way to mastery of the scriptwriting process!

"Hi my name is John, and I'm with this security company. I'm out talking to independent business owners who want to improve the productivity and profitability of their business operations. In this tough economy, crime is increasing, and new threats are quickly evolving. When we meet, you'll receive a customized crime report for your business address. This crime report focuses both on personal crime and property crime. Personal crime affects your safety and the safety of your employees. Property crime affects the physical safety of the business. When we meet, you'll also learn

some powerful ideas on ways to improve the profitability of your business."

Let me share with you all the layers that are in this Appointment Setting Script.

"Independent business owners" This is a prequalification script. I can only work with independent business owners, mom and pops up to 25 employees. I cannot work with franchisees that were handled by a different department, so this is a very important prequalification script. If the business was a franchise, and there are a lot of franchises out there, I could move on to the next potential customer.

The script to smoke out the gatekeeper

"business owners who want to improve the productivity and profitability of their business operations." This script was designed to smoke out the gatekeeper, so I would be connected to the business owner. In this example, I'm speaking the language of the business owner and not just as a "salesperson."

Another advanced scripting technique I'm using here is *Hypnotic Repetition. Hypnotic repetition* is the key use of certain words or phrases over and over again throughout your presentation. You must remember to sprinkle these keywords or phrases throughout the presentation, so it does not come to the conscious awareness of your prospect. Don't be afraid to use this technique; it is one of the most powerful techniques you have available as a sales professional. In the appointment setting script above, there are several keywords or phrases that are used hypnotically. Can you find them?

We have used the word "crime" three times and the word "security" two times.

We will also used the benefits of taking action and the consequences of not taking action scripts.

In this tough economy, crime is increasing, and new threats are quickly evolving. When we meet, you'll receive a customized crime report for your business address. This crime report focuses both on personal crime and property crime. Personal crime affects your safety and the safety of your employees. Property crime affects the physical safety of the business.

Note, both the benefits of taking action and the consequences of not taking action are all implied in this script. The benefits of taking action are the sooner they take action, they can protect themselves, employees, and property from crime and those quickly evolving threats. The consequences of not taking action are also implied here. If their business gets robbed, they could get hurt or one of their employees could get hurt, and if an employee gets hurt, you'll probably have a lawsuit; nor do they want their property vandalized.

The *Curiosity Script*: a Free Report

A Free Report

A free report is a powerful tool to get people to meet with you for an appointment. The free report is only a few pages long and has to be of interest to your prospect. If the prospect is sitting on the fence and not quite sure to meet with you, the free report can be that little nudge that gets him to agree to the appointment. A free report is not a book! A free report has powerful information that is helpful to the prospect and does not tell the whole story. A free report will help you to book more appointments and thus close more sales. Create a customized free report for your business as soon as you can.

They will only be able to see the free report if they meet with me. Now remember, a free report does not have to be very long; it could be a couple of pages that helps establish your credibility. In this case, the free report was a one-page color-coded map with the business in the center of the map at "ground zero." The surrounding areas were color-coded by levels of crime. A yellow crime area is of concern; an orange crime area is of great concern, and a red crime area means: get out of town as soon as you can!

Master scripting and scripting techniques and when you layer them together, your scripts will become even more powerful and more persuasive.

CHAPTER 21

12 Specific Scripting Techniques and How to Use Them

12 Essential Scripting Techniques

A Leading Language, People Believe What They Say, Not What You Say

Leading Language is a powerful technique in your scripting toolkit. Why is it so important? Because people believe what they say, not what you say. People are inherently skeptical of what other people say, which includes salespeople. People don't deliberately lie to themselves, so if you get prospects to say what you want them to say, it has a deeper level of impact. Here's a quick example: *"If you want to get better at playing the piano, how do you get better at playing the piano?"* The prospect will respond with "You practice." This is the power of *leading language.*

1. An Undeniable Truth

An undeniable truth is a statement that everyone can agree with. What this does is to start developing trust and rapport with your prospect. An undeniable truth is especially important in a cold-calling type of situation because the person doesn't know you at all. When you use an undeniable truth, he can agree with you. You are starting to get agreement from the very beginning.

2. Connect the Known to the Unknown

Connecting the known to the unknown is a scripting technique to help prospects understand the key concepts of what you're selling. If the prospect does not understand a key concept, he will not be able to move forward and make a buying decision. The following is an example of connecting the known to the unknown:

Part of selling is education. One way to educate people is to connect something they know the something that they don't know.

There are many anti-oxidant health products being sold today. Oxidation is harmful. How would you explain oxidation in a way to a prospect that he can easily understand? By **Connecting the Known to the Unknown**.

Here's an example:

"Think of finding a bright new shiny penny. It glows almost a fiery red copper color in the sun. [Pause] Now think

of finding a penny that has been outside for many years. It is a sickly green color because the penny has turned from red to green from oxidation. Oxidation breaks things down. Oxidation in your body breaks down your cells. That is why anti-oxidants are so important for your general health." [Pause]

3. Define Your Terms

Defining your terms is essential to successful communication. Jargon or industry terminology often creeps into sales presentations which ultimately confuses the prospect. Prospects who are embarrassed and don't know something rarely buy. First, you should avoid industry jargon whenever possible. If you have to use the term, be sure you define it with the prospect so both of you are on the same page throughout the presentation. Something as common as a 401(k) needs to be described and defined; otherwise, you and the prospect will be having two different "conversations" about what a 401(k) means.

4. Getting Permission

Getting permission from a prospect to proceed is an effective tool; however, it must not be overused. Many salespeople ask for permission too many times during the presentation which ultimately diminishes the effectiveness of the presentation. People buy confidence! If you're asking permission too many times throughout the presentation, your prospect starts to get worried and does not buy. The best time to ask for permission is early in the presentation! Once you have received permission, it is not necessary to ask for it again.

"In order for me to best help you, _____ [prospects name] I need to ask a few questions about your situation. Would that be okay?"

Asking for permission at the questioning section of your presentation is a perfect time to ask for it. After that, it is usually not necessary to ask for it again.

5. Perfect Practice Makes Perfect

You want to rehearse your presentation and your scripts so you can deliver them perfectly. Jack Nicklaus, the world-famous golfer, was asked if practice makes perfect. His response was: *"Perfect practice makes perfect."* When you have prepared to deliver your scripts at this level, at any time you can deliver an excellent presentation. You must be ready at any time to deliver a perfect presentation which gives you the best chance of closing the sale.

6.Relevancy

Make sure what you are saying is relevant to your prospect. This is an important technique to make your sales presentation as efficient and as effective as possible. Ask yourself this question: *"Is this sentence in my sales presentation relevant to my prospect's needs and wants?"* If it is not relevant, delete it from your presentation. Sales presentations that contain too much information and are too long lose sales. A sales presentation that is too short, on the other hand, does not contain enough relevant information for the prospect to make a buying decision.

7. Reverse Engineering

Reverse engineering is what Stephen Covey talks about in his book, <u>The Seven Habits of Highly Effective People</u>. It talks about "Begin with the end in mind." What this means is start at the end of your presentation and work yourself to the beginning. Then every part of your sales presentation will be aligned with your outcome which is to make the sale. You have to reverse engineer every single script that you write. If you don't, you're back to winging-it again, and you'll get wing-it results.

8. The "yes" set

The "yes" *set* is also known as the accumulated *yes* technique. The strategy behind this is to elicit many small "yeses" throughout the presentation which makes the prospect more likely to give you the big "yes" at the end. Sprinkle the "yeses" throughout your presentation for the greatest effect. Do not use more than one accumulated yes per 4 minutes of presentation time. Greater frequency and the technique becomes obvious to the conscious mind of your prospect, and it loses its effectiveness.

9. Artfully Vague Language

Politicians are masters of the Artfully Vague Language scripting technique. Artfully vague language allows the prospects to project what is most important to them on to the words that are being said. In some cases, the prospects may not know specifically what they want, but we want to elicit from them general feelings. For example, financial service providers need to help their clients get connected to what a retirement looks like for them. Many people have not thought in specific detail what their retirement will look like 20 years in the future; nevertheless, the financial service provider must elicit this type of information so that the client can get connected to what a wonderful retirement would look like. This is an example of artfully vague language: *"Imagine your retirement without any money worries and having the freedom to do whatever you want whenever you want. What would that look like to you?"*

10. Experiential Involvement

Getting people involved with your product or service is essential. You can tell people about your product or service all you want; however, when you get them further involved, they will take ownership of it. That's why product demonstrations followed by the customer using the product is such a powerful selling technique. Test-driving a new car is an essential part of the sales process because the potential owner must feel comfortable with how the car handles; in fact, the sales professional will be explaining to the prospect how easy the car is to drive while the person is test-driving it. This experiential involvement is a key component of this particular type of sale. Think about how you can use experiential involvement product-demonstration in your sales presentation.

11. Contrast Script

People can make decisions to buy when they see the contrast between two alternatives, usually a positive alternative and a negative alternative. By focusing on this contrast, the person can make a buying decision because he doesn't want the negative outcome; he wants a positive outcome. Contrast scripts are used effectively in selling insurance. The insurance agent paints a picture of what would happen to their family without the life insurance and then will contrast it with how life insurance could help the family in case of an untimely death of the primary breadwinner. This is a powerful way to use contrast. It is okay to paint a negative picture with a prospect because you are providing this solution to that problem.

12. Free Report

A free report is a powerful tool to get people to meet with you for an appointment. The free report is only a few pages long and has to be of interest to your prospect. If the prospect is sitting on the fence and not quite sure to meet with you, the free report can be that little nudge that gets him to agree to the appointment. A free report is not a book! A free report has powerful information that is helpful to the prospect and does not tell the whole story. A free report will help you to book more appointments and thus close more sales. Create a customized free report for your business as soon as you can.

CHAPTER 22

Invisible Script

"Are Your Scripts Invisible?"

The Invisible Script

The highest level of script delivery is when it is totally invisible to the prospect. Think of like an actor or actress; each literally becomes the script. That is why the best paid actors and actresses are so persuasive is because they have become their scripts.

CHAPTER 23

Special Offer

I want to acknowledge you today for investing the time to learn about how to transform your salespeople into a Sales Force. By implementing the *Scripting Secrets* in this book, you're well on your way to developing *Sales Scripts* and a Sales Force that is one of the most powerful in your industry.

Now, I'm extending to you an invitation to learn more about how sales scripting can help transform your business.

Because you have invested your time to read this book, I want to share another powerful resource with you.

You are eligible for a free 30-minute, no cost or obligation telephone consultation, when I can share with you the powerful ways to customize your *Sales Scripts* and start the process of transforming your sales department into a Sales Force.

To reserve your free 30-minute telephone consultation, call Tel: **714-688-6443**.

You may also fax the <u>Critique Certificate</u> below to:

Fax: 714-846-8619

$250.00   Sales Script Critique Certificate $250.00

Entitles bearer to a complimentary, 30-minute telephone consultation when submitting any single *Sales Script* for verbal critique from John Kurth.

Name

_____

Company (if any)

_____

Address

_____

_____

City, State, Zip

_____

Phone _____ Fax _____

Email Address

_____

Send Certificate and Materials to:

John Kurth

President

Syntactics Sales Scripting®

The Syntax of Success®

5942 Edinger Ave.

Suite 113, PMB 323

Huntington Beach, CA 92649

Fax: 714-846-8619

Call Tel: (714) 688-6443 to schedule a 30-minute Telephone Script Review.

John Kurth

President

Syntactics Sales Scripting™

The Syntax of Success™

5942 Edinger Ave.

Suite 113, PMB 323

Huntington Beach, CA 92649

Terms and Conditions:

Certificate expires 6 months from the date of book

purchase. Consultation will be given by telephone only. Actual finished Sales Script materials or "rough drafts" may be discussed. Coupon redeemable only for Sales Scripting Services. Additional consulting may be contracted for, Mr. Kurth's schedule permitting. Fees quoted on request.

Call (714) 688-6443 to set up an appointment.

CPSIA information can be obtained
at www.ICGtesting.com
Printed in the USA
FSOW02n0923290416
19864FS